A FIELD GUIDE TO
BOSTON
MASSACHUSETTS

PHOTOGRAPHY BY KEVIN AND SUSAN PSAROS
NARRATIVE BY NICHOLE WADSWORTH SCHRAFFT

Copyright © 2009 by
Twin Lights Publishers, Inc.

All rights reserved. No part of this book may be reproduced in any form without written permission of the copyright owners. All images in this book have been reproduced with the knowledge and prior consent of the artists concerned and no responsibility is accepted by producer, publisher, or printer for any infringement of copyright or otherwise, arising from the contents of this publication. Every effort has been made to ensure that credits accurately comply with information supplied.

First published in the United States of America by:

Twin Lights Publishers, Inc.
8 Hale Street
Rockport, Massachusetts 01966
Telephone: (978) 546-7398
http://www.twinlightspub.com

ISBN 978-1-885435-95-8
ISBN 1-885435-95-9

10 9 8 7 6 5 4 3 2 1

Book design by
SYP Design & Production, Inc.
http://www.sypdesign.com

Printed in China

INTRODUCTION

Call it what you will—Boston, Beantown, the Cradle of America, the Hub, the Walking City, capital of Red Sox Nation, or the City-with-no-"r's"—no matter what the name, Boston is one spectacular city.

My own relationship with the city of Boston has recently come full circle. As a child growing up on the North Shore, trips to Boston were very exciting occasions. Many a weekend was spent feeding the pigeons in the Boston Common and some of my favorite, old home movies depict happy days on the swan boats.

As a teenager, Boston had a different version of fun awaiting me. A typical day then consisted of a train ride to North Station, a stop in Faneuil Hall for a chocolate croissant at Au Bon Pain, a brisk walk to Downtown Crossing for some shopping, and then a "T" ride across the Charles to Harvard Square and a visit to the Coop, Urban Outfitters, and Pizzeria Regina.

Now, just this past weekend, my husband and I proudly brought our one-year-old to Boston Common and we even fed some pigeons.

One thing is different now, however. As an adult, a teacher, and a mom, I can greatly appreciate another side of the city. The historical significance of this city is unlike any other. The opportunities to find a lesson to teach or a story to share are around each and every corner and the effect that Boston has had on the rest of our great country is undeniable.

May this book be your guide as you navigate your way through Boston's cobblestone streets, waterfront locations, towering skyscrapers, meandering greenways, culturally-rich neighborhoods, local markets, parks, museums, colleges, universities, and world-class teaching hospitals. While doing so, stop and listen carefully. You might just hear the clip-clop of Paul Revere's horse, the angelic voices of the children's choir signing the first *My Country 'Tis of Thee,* the splash of tea landing in the harbor, or the British troops evacuating the city. Then again, it may just be the fans over at Fenway Park cheering on their team.

—Nichole Wadsworth Schraff

Acorn Street

A beautiful and historic cobblestone street found in Boston's Beacon Hill Area. Acorn Street is one of the most photographed streets in Boston as well as the United States.

Adams, Abigail

Abigail Smith was born in Weymouth, Massachusetts. She was the wife of President John Adams and the mother of President John Quincy Adams. Abigail spent the last 17 years of her life living in Quincy, Massachusetts.

Adams, John

Born in Braintree, Massachusetts in 1735, John Adams attended Harvard University and became a lawyer. Later, as a member of the Massachusetts Assembly, he represented Massachusetts at the First Continental Congress. In 1789 he became the first Vice President of the United States under George Washington and in 1796 he became the second United States President. He retired to Quincy, Massachusetts until his death on the 4th of July, 1826, the 50 year anniversary of the Declaration of Independence.

AMERICA

This song, more commonly known as *My County 'Tis of Thee*, was first sung at the Park Street Church in Boston on July 4th, 1831 by a children's choir.

AMERICAN REVOLUTION

A series of events, including the Revolutionary War, that led to the separation of the 13 original British colonies in America from Britian as well as the the formation of the United States of America. Some of the major events of the Revolution were the Boston Massacre, the Boston Tea Party, the First and Second Continental Congresses, the Battles of Lexington and Concord, Fort Ticonderoga, the British Evacuation of Boston, and the signing of the Declaration of Independence.

AMTRAK

A system of passenger trains that run throughout the country. The name was created by using pieces of the words "American" and "track." Most of the Amtrak trains in Boston run in and out of South Station.

ADAMS, SAMUEL

The third Lieutenant Governor and fourth Governor of Massachusetts. He was an important and controversial leader in the fight for the rights of the American Colonists. Though John and Samuel were cousins, they were often referred to as the Adams' brothers. A statue of Samuel Adams stands on Congress Street by Faneuil Hall.

August Moon Festival

A festival celebrated in Boston's China Town each August. The actual August Moon Festival takes place on the 15th day of the 8th lunar month (August 15th). Chinese legend says the moon is the fullest and brightest on that day. Pastries called moon pies are the most traditional and famous treat enjoyed during the festival.

Apollo Commander

As you walk through the Museum of Science it is impossible to miss the *Apollo Command Module*. To see more, visit the rest of the Earth and Space Study exhibits, shows, and the planetarium.

Auerbach, Red

The first NBA coach to draft an African-American, and the first to present an all-black starting five. Auerbach was part of the Celtics family for 57 years and guided them to 16 championships. He was inducted into the Basketball Hall of Fame in 1969. This statue is located in Faneuil Hall Marketplace.

B

Back Bay

One of the many neighborhoods that make up Boston. The Back Bay is best known for its expensive homes and shopping. The area was under water until 1857, when 400 acres of new land were created by filling in mud flats of the Charles River.

Barking Crab

A seafood restaurant located alongside Boston's Four Point Channel. The Barking Crab opened in 1994 as a summer seafood spot and after two seasons was such a huge hit that it began to operate year round. They'll tell you they offer "the casual atmosphere of a coastal clam shack in a funky urban setting."

Baseball

A sport played by two teams using a bat and ball that began around the year 1845, with a list of rules written by Alexander Cartwright. The first professional games were played around 1865. The Boston Red Sox lead all other Major League Baseball teams with attendance to their road games, and have continually sold out their home games since 2003.

Beacon Hill

A famous neighborhood in Boston. Beacon Hill has brick and cobblestone sidewalks and streets lit by gas lamps. The State House is located at the top of Beacon Hill. The hill was once a lot higher, but was made smaller to make it easier to build new homes. The extra land was used to help create the Back Bay area.

Beacon Street

A street that runs through Boston, Brookline, Brighton, and Newton. Beacon Street is most famous where it joins with Beacon Hill and the State House. It then runs through the Back Bay, into Kenmore Square, and past Fenway Park before leaving the city of Boston.

Beantown

The nickname given to the city of Boston because of its history of baking beans in molasses during the colonial times.

Beantown Trolley

A popular sightseeing tour enjoyed by tourists, and even locals, who want to learn more about the city of Boston. The trolley tour welcomes passengers to hop on and off allowing as much time as they would like at each of the 20 stops. A new trolley comes along every 20 minutes for riders who have stayed behind.

Bell in Hand Tavern

A tavern opened in 1795 and located on Union Street in Boston. The Bell in Hand is the oldest continuously operating tavern in all of America.

Benjamin Franklin's Statue

The first portrait statue in America. It stands in front of the Old City Hall on School Street. The statue overlooks the site of America's first public school where Benjamin Franklin attended. His birthplace is just one block away. Surrounding the bottom of the statue are four bronze tablets that represent Franklin's careers as a printer, scientist, and the signer of both the Declaration of Independence and the Peace Treaty with France.

Big Dig

A nickname given to a huge construction project, officially named "The Central Artery/Tunnel Project," that has improved some of Boston's major roadways. The Ted William's Tunnel and the beautiful Zakim Bridge are results of this enormous project that started in 1991 and cost 14.6 million dollars. It is the most expensive United States Highway Project in history.

Bird, Larry

A former NBA basketball player who played for 13 seasons with the Boston Celtics until he left in 1992. That summer, Larry Bird played with the United States "Dream Team" helping win a gold medal during the Barcelona, Spain Olympics. The Celtics retired his jersey number, 33, upon his departure from the team.

Black Heritage Trail

A 14-stop walking tour that explores the 19th-century life of Boston's African American Community.

Blackstone, Reverend William

The first European to settle in Boston. Blackstone sailed to New England with an expedition in 1623. When the others returned to England, he stayed behind and lived in what is now the Beacon Hill area of Boston. Blackstone later moved to a hill that he named *Study Hill* where he read books, planted gardens, and took care of cattle for 40 years. The hill overlooks a river that is now named the Blackstone River after the Reverend.

Blue Man Group

A unique show that combines music, acting, and comedy to create a really exciting stage experience.

Boston

The capital of Massachusetts. Boston was founded in 1630 by about 1000 Puritan colonists of the Massachusetts Bay Company. Today, the population of Boston is around 560,000.

Boston Accent

A famously distinct way of speaking Bostonians seem to have that is widely poked fun at. It is said that people from Boston don't pronounce the letter *r*. A common example is "*Pahk the cah in Havahd Yahd.*"

Boston Children's Museum

An interactive and educational museum for children located in South Boston.

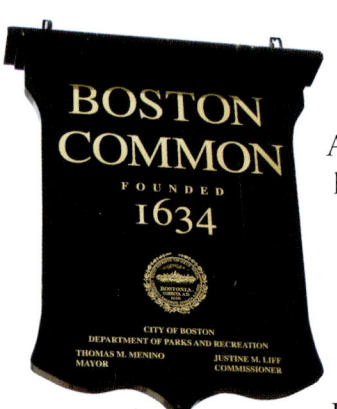

Boston Common

A 50-acre park located in the middle of Boston. One of the first stops along the Freedom Trail, Boston Common is the oldest city park in the country. The park has many fun attractions such as the Frog Pond skating rink, the Parkman Bandstand, softball fields, statues, and an annual Christmas Tree.

Boston Fire Museum

A museum dedicated to preserving the history of Boston's Fire Departments. The museum is full of photographs, memorabilia, and fire fighting equipment.

Boston Globe

Boston's most circulated newspaper. The first paper was published in 1872 and sold for 4 cents.

Boston Harbor

The body of water that allows boat traffic to enter the city. Dorchester, Quincy, and Hingham Bays come together to form the outer harbor. Ferries, sightseeing boats, whale watches, coast guard vessels, tugboats, cargo ships, and even cruise ships can be seen going in and out of Boston's harbor. Several islands can also be found within the harbor's waters.

Boston Harbor Islands National Park

The 34 islands found in Boston Harbor make up this national park. Visitors can hike, camp, fish, swim, picnic, or just relax. The park is home to Graves Light, Long Island Head Light, and Boston Light. Boston Light is the oldest and first lighthouse site in the United States.

Boston Latin School

The oldest public school in the country. Located along the Freedom Trail, Boston Latin opened in 1635 as an all boy's school. It is now coeducational and has over 2,000 students.

Boston Marathon

A 26.2-mile race run each Patriot's Day through Boston and neighboring cities. The race begins in Hopkinton and ends on Boylston Street in Boston, in front of the Boston Public Library. Runners travel from all around the globe to participate in the world's oldest annual marathon. Runners can first spot the finish line as they round a corner 3 ½ blocks away.

Boston Massacre

The name given to an incident that occurred on May 5, 1770 between a group of Boston citizens and British soldiers. Social tension escalated into a riot between civilians and British troops, which ended in five civilians being killed. The men are buried at the Granary Burial Ground on Tremont Street. A cobblestone marker at the actual site of the massacre is located in front of the Old State House on State Street along Boston's Freedom Trail.

Boston Pops

A group of musicians from the larger Boston Symphony Orchestra. The "Pops" was founded in 1885 with hopes of performing lighter music than the more traditional orchestra performs. Today, the "Pops" are probably best known for playing in the annual 4th of July show on the Esplanade.

Boston Post Road

A system of roads that ran between Boston and New York. The original roads were paths used by post riders and their horses. Some of the milestones used to mark the original roads can still be seen along the route today.

Boston Public Library

The first large library in the country to be open to the public and to allow people to check out books. When the library opened in 1854 it had 16,000 books. Today, it is estimated to have 17.5 million, making it one of the largest in the country.

Boston Symphony Hall

Home to the Boston Symphony Orchestra and the Boston Pops. Thanks to its fabulous acoustics Boston Symphony Hall is rated in the top three in the entire world.

Boston Tea Party Ship and Museum

A museum whose purpose is to preserve the history of the Boston Tea Party. The museum is part of the Historic Tours of America. The *Beaver II*, one of the ships found at the Boston Tea Party Museum, is a replica of one of the original Boston Tea Party Ships.

Boston University

The fourth largest university in the United States. Boston University has close to 30,000 students and covers 132 acres in the city of Boston. "The Terriers" is the athletic teams' nickname and their colors are scarlet and white.

Bostonian

The name given to a citizen of Boston.

Bruins

Boston's professional hockey team. The Boston Bruins is one of the six original teams of the National Hockey League (NHL). Their home games are played at the TD Banknorth Garden. Since their founding in 1924, the Bruins have won 5 Stanley Cup championships.

Bull and Finch Pub

Located on Beacon Street in Boston, the Bull and Finch Pub was the inspiration for the television show *Cheers*, which first aired in 1982.

Bunker Hill Monument

A 221-foot-tall granite pillar built to commemorate the Battle of Bunker Hill. Located on Breed's Hill, the monument is the first obelisk erected in the United States. An obelisk is a tall four-sided stone pillar that gets narrower as it gets taller with the top shaping into a pyramid. The Bunker Hill Monument is one of several historical sites along Boston's Freedom Trail. Visitors who want to climb to the top have to climb 294 steps, but the view is worth it.

C

Callahan Tunnel

A tunnel that travels underneath Boston Harbor and carries traffic from the North End of Boston towards Logan Airport and East Boston. At 5,069 feet the tunnel is just under one mile long. Its full name is The Lieutenant William F. Callahan Tunnel and it was opened in 1961.

Cambridge

A city located across the Charles River from Boston. Cambridge is well known for being the home to Harvard University.

Cannoli

An Italian pastry. A cannoli is made from fried pastry dough that is rolled into a tube and then filled with, most typically, ricotta cheese. The ends of the cannoli are sometimes flavored with things like pistachios, bits of chocolate, or sprinkles.

Castle Island

A 22-acre island that is now attached to the mainland in South Boston. Castle Island is open for tours during the summer months and is also home to the five-sided Fort Independence. Castle Island and Fort Independence were in the perfect location to protect the city of Boston during the War of 1812.

Celtics

The professional basketball team that calls Boston home. The Boston Celtics play in the TD Banknorth Garden on the famous parquet floor. The Celtics have been World Champions a record making 16 times. No other team in the NBA (National Basketball Association) has won as many titles as Boston's home team.

CENTRAL ARTERY

The major highway that runs through Boston. Until the Big Dig began, the Central Artery traveled above ground between the waterfront and downtown area. The Big Dig's plan moved the Central Artery under ground.

CHARLES RIVER

The river that separates the city of Boston from its neighbors, Charlestown and Cambridge. The river starts in Hopkinton, flows through 58 of Massachusett's towns, enters Boston, and then empties into Boston Harbor.

CHARLESTOWN NAVY YARD

Home to the USS *Constitution* and the Boston National Historical Park. The Navy Yard was first opened in 1801 and was officially closed in 1974. Before being closed it was one of the Navy's oldest ship-building yards.

CHARLIE PASS

A card used to pay fares when riding the cities subways and buses.

CHILTON, MARY

The first woman to step off of the *Mayflower* and onto Plymouth Rock. Mary made the voyage with her mother and father. Mary's father passed away while the *Mayflower* was still docked in Provincetown, and her mother died during the first long, hard winter in Plymouth. Mary was later married to John Winslow and they moved to Boston after the birth of their 10th child.

CHINATOWN

An area of Boston that is home to a large Asian population as well as many Asian markets, shops, and restaurants. A large gate called a *paifang* stands at one of the entrances.

CHRISTIAN SCIENCE CHURCH

A religious denomination started in 1879 by Mary Baker Eddy. Today, there are over 2,000 Christian Science Churches found around the world. The headquarters, the First Church of Christ, Scientist, is located in Boston.

CHRISTOPHER COLUMBUS WATERFRONT PARK

Boston's first waterfront park. Located in the North End, visitors can enjoy a beautiful view of the working waterfront along with a rose garden, play area, fountain, and a statue of Christopher Columbus.

CITGO SIGN

A large neon sign that has hovered above Kenmore Square since 1965. It was scheduled to be removed in 1983, but the people of Boston rallied to save it. The sign measures 60 feet by 60 feet and contains more than 5 miles of neon tubes.

CLAM CHOWDER

A thick soup made with a milk or cream base and, of course, clams. Bostonians take their clam chowder, or "chowda," very seriously and several competitions are held each year to find Boston's very best clam chowders. Not everyone agrees on which recipe is the best, however, mostly everyone agrees clam chowder is one of Boston's most famous foods.

COMMONWEALTH AVENUE

One of Boston's most beautiful streets. "Comm. Ave," as it is often called, begins in the Back Bay area of Boston. This first section of the street is lined with large multi-story brownstone buildings with a grassy area in the middle of the east and westbound lanes. The grassy area is called the Commonwealth Avenue Mall and consists of more than 8 acres. The street continues through Boston, Allston, Brighton, Chestnut Hill, Newton, and Weston.

Commonwealth of Mass

The official name for Massachusetts. The definition of *commonwealth* is "an organized territory that has established a more highly developed relationship with the Federal government." The United States is actually made up of 46 states and 4 commonwealths. While the 4 commonwealths can be called states, the other 46 states cannot be called commonwealths.

Coop

A Harvard University bookstore located in Cambridge's Harvard Square.

Copley Square

Located in Boston's Back Bay area, Copley Square is known for its shopping, hotels, and restaurants. It is home to the Boston Public Library and hosts outdoor concerts during warm weather months.

Copp's Hill Burying Ground

Boston's second oldest burying ground. Copp's Hill Burying Ground is one of many historic sites along Boston's Freedom Trail. The land was once owned by a shoemaker named William Copp.

Courthouse

The John Joseph Moakley United States Courthouse serves as the headquarters for the United States Court of Appeals for the First Circuit and the United States District Court for Massachusetts. There are two courtrooms for the Court of Appeals and 25 individual courtrooms for the District Court. It also houses the offices of a U.S. Congressman and the U.S. Attorney General, 40 judges' chambers, a law library, and U.S. Marshals Service facilities.

Cradle of Liberty

A name given to Boston because of its involvement in the start of the American Revolution.

Crew

The sport of rowing. On any given day rowers can be seen up and down the Charles River. Crew teams from colleges and universities such as Harvard, MIT, Boston University, Boston College, Brandeis, Wellesley, and Northeastern use the river. Many local crew clubs, local high schools, and individuals enjoy crew as a hobby and sport. The Head of the Charles Regatta is the world's largest two-day rowing event and takes place each October on the Charles River.

Custom House

Boston's first skyscraper. The original Custom House, built in 1849, sat on the waterfront before landfill extended the city of Boston. The Custom House was where maritime business took place and where the ship captains would pay their duties. In 1915 a 495-foot tower was added to make it even taller. Today, the Custom House is a beautiful hotel.

D

Dolphin Sculpture

The *Dolphins of the Sea* sculpture can be found on Central Wharf near the New England Aquarium. Boston-born artist, Katharine Lane Weems, studied the movements, behaviors, and anatomy of each animal prior to creating her pieces. Thirty pieces from her collection were donated to the Museum of Science while others, like the *Dolphins of the Sea*, can be seen throughout the city of Boston.

Downtown

Boston's financial and business district. Downtown is home to places such as Faneuil Hall, Quincy Market, Downtown Crossing, the Old State House, and the Old South Meeting House.

Duck Tours

The Boston Duck Tours use World War II amphibious landing vehicles (or DUKWs) to tour Boston by land before splashing into the Charles River to finish their 80 minute tours. Tour guides, appropriately called "conducktors" are full of fascinating information about historical and modern day Boston.

E

EMERALD NECKLACE

A series of 12 parks linked together throughout the city of Boston. The Emerald Necklace covers a distance of about seven miles from beginning to end with a total of 1,100 acres of land to be enjoyed by everyone.

ESPLANADE

The three-mile stretch of land along the banks of The Charles River between the Museum of Science and the Boston University Bridge. The Esplanade is enjoyed by residents and tourists in a variety of different ways including biking and walking paths, playgrounds, a wading pool, tennis courts, softball fields, soccer fields, boat docks, concession stands, and the Hatch Shell for concerts. The annual 4th of July fireworks are always one of the Esplanades biggest events.

EVACUATION DAY

On March 17th, 1776, in the midst of the Revolutionary War, British troops evacuated Boston. March 17th was declared Evacuation Day in the year 1941 and has been a legal holiday in Suffolk County ever since.

F

FAMOUS BOSTON MUSICIANS

Many musicians got their start in the great city of Boston and the surrounding area. The bands Aerosmith, Boston, and The Cars along with James Taylor, Donna Summer, and Jo Dee Messina are just a few examples of great musicians who have come from Boston.

FAMOUS PEOPLE

Many famous people have called Boston home. Writers, actors, politicians, athletes, and many more have hailed from this historic city. John Fitzgerald Kennedy, Christa McAuliffe, Eli Whitney, Ralph Waldo Emerson, Leonard Nemoy, Dr. Suess, Winslow Homer, Bette Davis, F. Lee Bailey, Emily Dickinson, and Benjamin Franklin are just a few famous individuals off of the long, long list.

Faneuil Hall

A building originally used as a forum for speakers and a marketplace for produce, meat, and fish vendors. Faneuil Hall was given to the city of Boston as a gift from Peter Faneuil in 1742. Today, Faneuil Hall is a part of Faneuil Hall Marketplace and is a favorite Boston destination along the Freedom Trail. The main hall is called Quincy Market and serves as a large food court. On either side of the food pavilion, vending carts and shops can be found.

Feast of St. Anthony

An annual celebration held in Boston's North End on the last weekend in August. The original Feast of St. Anthony takes place in Montefalcione, Italy, but as Italian immigrants from Montefalcione arrived in Boston's North End in 1919 they began to recreate the tradition in their new home. The weekend includes processions, music, live entertainment, marching bands, masses, serenaders, dancing, cooking demonstrations, contests, and, of course, a ton of food!

Fenway Park

Home to the Boston Red Sox. Fenway Park was opened in 1912 and is the oldest professional ballpark in the United States. It is called Fenway because it was built in the area of Boston known as the Fens.

Fiedler, Arthur

The conductor of the Boston Pops Orchestra from 1930-1979. Fiedler had many accomplishments in his professional career, one of which was conducting in the opening ceremonies of Walt Disney World in 1971. There is a statue of Arthur Fiedler near the Hatch Memorial Shell.

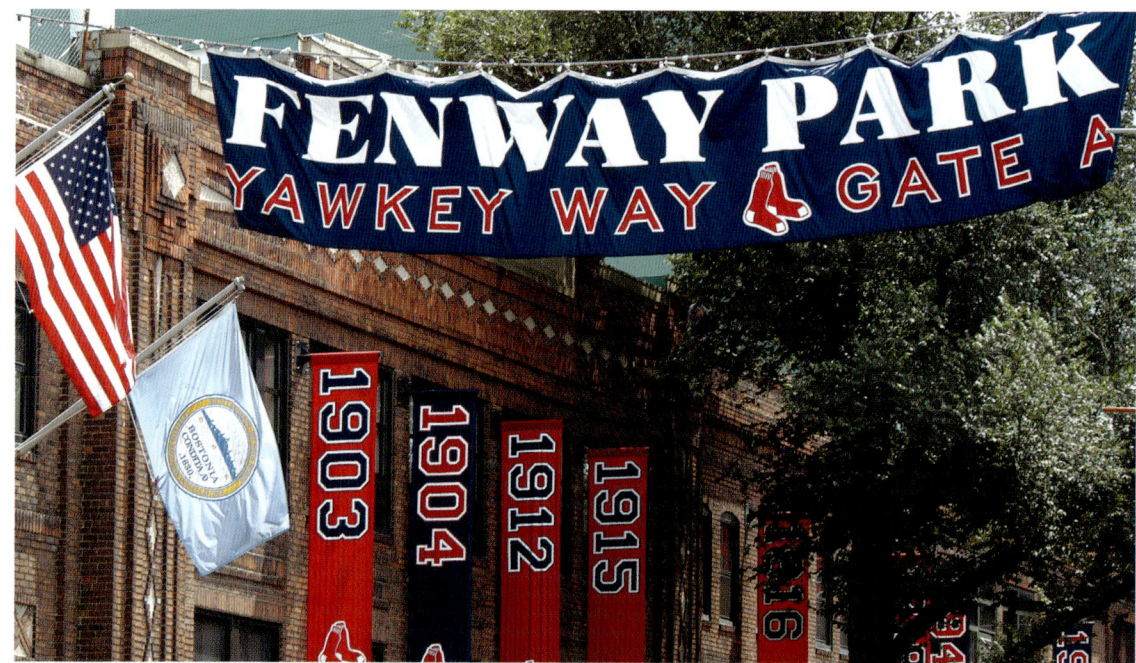

Fire Boat

A boat shaped a lot like a tugboat used to fight fires on the water and along the waterfront. Fire boats pump water directly from the ocean allowing for an unlimited supply of water and the ability to spray large amounts at once.

Fire Department

The approximately 1,600 men and women who dedicate themselves to keeping Boston safe from fire. Boston has 35 fire stations and the first paid department was started in 1678.

First Baptist Church

The third church established in Boston and the fifth Baptist Church to be formed in the entire country. The church was founded on June 7, 1665 by two women and seven men and is located on Commonwealth Avenue.

Fort Warren

Now a tourist attraction, Fort Warren was originally a jail for prisoners of war during the Civil War. Located on George's Island, at the entrance to Boston Harbor, Fort Warren was in the ideal place to help defend the city during World War I and World War II.

Firefighter

A person who works or volunteers with a fire department to fight fires. Firefighters report to fires, work on fire prevention, maintain equipment, conduct safety checks, and educate the public on fire safety.

Fountains

A structure that sprays water for splashing in or just for decoration. The fountains at the Frog Pond in Boston Common, at the Church of Christ, Scientist, and in Copley Square are all fun ways to cool off on hot summer days.

Franklin Park Zoo

A 72-acre zoo in Boston's Franklin Park. The zoo is home to all sorts of animals who live in exhibits called Serengeti Crossing, Franklin Farm, Kalahari Kingdom, Tiger Tales, Giraffe Savannah, Tropical Forest, Butterfly Landing, Bird's World, and the Outback Trail.

Freedom Trail

A 2 ½ mile red path that winds through downtown Boston. The Freedom Trail includes 16 historical locations along its route. People can walk the Freedom Trail alone or take a guided tour with a National Park Service Ranger.

Fresnel Lens

A lens developed for lighthouses by a man named Augustin-Jean Fresnel. The lenses are thinner and lighter than typical lighthouse lenses and consequently allow more light to pass through. The extra light means ships can spot lighthouses from farther away. Boston Light was updated with a 2nd Order Fresnel Lens in 1859.

Frog Pond

A wading pool complete with a spray fountain during warm weather months and a skating rink during the winter. The Boston Common Frog Pond offers year-round fun. Frog statues keep an eye on the excitement and the Tadpole Playground next door gives kids another place to run around.

G

Gargoyle

An architectural feature found on buildings that usually looks like a mythical creature or animal. If you search the city of Boston you'll find many gargoyles staring down at you.

Gelato Stand

The Italian word for ice cream, gelato is a frozen dessert that is thicker or denser than American ice cream because it is made with less air and usually with milk instead of cream. There are over 50 places where you can buy a gelato in and around the city of Boston, many of which can be found in Boston's Italian North End.

George's Island

A 39-acre island (53 acres at low tide) at the entrance of Boston Harbor. George's Island is home to Fort Warren and has a large boat dock, walking paths, picnic grounds, a parade ground, and a gravel beach.

Gibson House Museum

This preserved home of Boston's Gibson family allows visitors to step back in time to the late 19th and early 20th centuries to see what life was like for a well-to-do Boston family.

Golden dome

The top of the State House. The dome was designed by Charles Bulfinch. When it was first built it was made of shingles. It didn't take long for the dome to begin to leak during bad weather. In 1802 the dome was covered with copper, provided by Paul Revere, to prevent further leaking. Then, in 1874, it was finished with gold leaf to create the beautiful shimmer that can be seen today.

Government Center

A city square and plaza that is home to Boston's City Hall. Government Center also serves as a "T" stop and is a favorite spot for outdoor concerts and events during warm weather months.

Granary Burying Ground

The city's third oldest cemetery, founded in 1660. Located on Tremont Street along Boston's Freedom Trail, the Granary is the final resting place for many famous people, including Samuel Adams, Peter Faneuil, John Hancock, and Paul Revere.

Grasshopper

The weathervane that sits on top of Faneuil Hall. Peter Faneuil received the copper grasshopper vane as a gift in 1742 from a Boston coppersmith named Shem Drowne. The roof of Faneuil Hall and the grasshopper were later made gold.

Green Monster

The name given to the left field wall in Boston's Fenway Park. The wall was part of the original ballpark, however, it wasn't until 1947 that it was painted green and given it's new nickname. The "Green Monster" is 37 feet and 2 inches high and is 310 feet from home plate when measured along the left field foul line. The wall is actually a manually operated scoreboard which also displays the scores of other games going on in both the American and National Leagues. The Green Monster seats were added atop the wall in 2003 and are now some of the hardest seats to get.

Hancock Tower

The tallest building in New England. The John Hancock Tower measures 790 feet tall and is 60 stories high. It is made of 10,344 panes of ½ inch thick glass windows. Near the Hancock Tower is the old John Hancock Building. It is known for the weather forecast beacon that sits on top of its roof. The well-known saying goes, "steady blue, clear view; flashing blue, clouds are due; steady red, rain ahead; flashing red, snow instead."

Hancock, John

Born in Braintree, Massachusetts, he became the first and third Governor of Massachusetts and President of the Second Continental Congress. He was also the first person to sign the Declaration of Independence. His signature was the largest and most noticeable on the document. Today, when people ask for a signature they may say, "Can I have your John Hancock?"

Harborwalk

A public walkway along Boston's waterfront that will be an amazing 46.9 miles when completed. It winds through the waterfront neighborhoods and Boston's downtown, stretching from Chelsea Creek to the Neponset River. The Harborwalk includes several parks, pieces of art, seating and picnic areas, cafés, water transportation facilities, and much more. The Harborwalk will eventually link together with the Emerald Necklace, the Charles River Esplanade, and the Rose Kennedy Greenway.

Harrison Gray Otis House

Located on Cambridge Street, this home was designed by Charles Bulfinch for Harrison Gray Otis. It is now a museum dedicated to showing the lavish life led by Boston's governing class. Harrison Gray Otis was responsible for the development of Boston's Beacon Hill, served as a Representative to Congress, and was eventually Mayor of Boston.

Harvard Square

An area next to Harvard University in Cambridge that is full of shops and restaurants. The square also has a "T" stop on the red line and is a favorite place for street performers to show off their talents.

Harvard University

The oldest university in the United States and a member of the Ivy League. Harvard was founded in 1636 and is located in Cambridge. The university has a long list of famous graduates, including Presidents John F. Kennedy and George W. Bush.

Hatch Memorial Shell

A concert stage located along the Charles River on Boston's Esplanade. The Hatch Shell has a huge domed roof which is completely open on one end. Used for concerts during the summer, the Hatch Shell is probably most famous for hosting the Boston Pops every July 4th.

Haymarket

A large outdoor market where fruits, vegetables, fish, and herbs are sold from carts and tables. Haymarket is known for its great prices and fresh foods.

Holocaust Memorial

Six large glass towers that represent the six concentration camps in operation during the Holocaust and dedicated to those who were held prisoner or lost their lives within one of the camps. On Holocaust Remembrance Day in 1993 a time capsule bearing names of friends and family members submitted by New Englanders was buried at the Memorial Site. The registration numbers of victims are etched in glass and quotes from survivors are carved in concrete.

Head of the Charles Regatta

A rowing race held on the Charles River each October. The Head of the Charles is the largest regatta in the world with about 8,000 rowers and over 1,500 boats. Rowers of all ages come from all around the world to participate.

Hood Milk Bottle

Built in 1933 in Taunton, Massachusetts, this outdoor ice cream stand is located in front of the Boston Children's Museum. It is 40 feet tall, has an 18 foot diameter at its base, and can hold 50,000 gallons of milk.

Hooker, Major General Joseph

A Major General in the Union Army during the Civil War. He was given the nickname "Fighting Joe" during his career. Major General Joseph Hooker was born in Hadley, Massachusetts and now a statue stands in his honor outside of the State House in Boston.

Horse & Carriage

A fantastic way to see Boston. Horse drawn carriages or hansom cabs can be taken around Boston Common, Faneuil Hall, the Back Bay, and parts of downtown Boston.

Horticultural Society

Horticulture is the science and art of growing flowers, fruit, plants, and vegetables in small gardens using simple tools. The Massachusetts Horticultural Society started with exhibits held in Faneuil Hall and Quincy Market displaying locally grown fruit and vegetables. They also taught the newest horticultural techniques and introduced new breeds and varieties of produce. The Concord grape was introduced at one of these exhibits in 1853.

Hutchinson, Anne

A controversial Puritan preacher who was later banished from her colony for preaching her own religious philosophy. She was an advocate of religious freedom and woman's rights. A statue of Anne Hutchinson and her daughter, Susannah, stands in front of the State House.

Hynes Convention Center

A building used for meetings, conventions, expositions, and events. The Hynes Convention Center, in Boston's Back Bay, hosts a wide variety of events each year.

I

IMMIGRATION

To leave ones home country and permanently move to another. Once the potato famine struck Ireland in the 1840s a large number of the population immigrated to the United States and settled primarily in Boston.

INDEPENDENCE DAY

A federal holiday that celebrates the adoption of The Declaration of Independence and the independence of the original 13 colonies from Great Britain's government. Independence Day falls on the 4th of July.

INNING

A part of a baseball game. An inning is a period of time that allows both teams a chance at bat. Once the batting team has earned three outs, one half of the inning is over and that team plays the field. If the score is tied at the end of nine innings, the game goes into extra innings until a winning team emerges. In 1981, the Pawtucket Red Sox played in the longest game in history. That game lasted 33 innings!

INSTITUTE OF CONTEMPORARY ART

The first museum in the country dedicated completely to contemporary art. Since 1936, the museum has presented modern forms of literature, film and video, performance, and visual art forms.

IRISH

One of the largest ethnic groups in Boston, mostly living in South Boston. After leaving Ireland in the 1840s the Irish flooded Boston, soon dominating politics and commerce. Boston is said to be the largest Irish city in America.

ISABELLA STEWART GARDNER MUSEUM

A museum that was opened in 1903 by Isabella Stewart Gardner. The museum is three stories high with galleries full of paintings, sculptures, tapestries, rare books, and furnishings from around the world. A beautiful courtyard is in the middle of the museum.

Jellyfish

Commonly mistaken for fish, these sea jellies do not have a backbone, heart, or brain, and are mostly water. Of the approximate 2,000 species of sea jellies only 70 are known to be harmful to humans. Thousands of jellies can be viewed at the Amazing Jellies exhibit at the New England Aquarium.

JFK Library and Museum

A tribute to the life and leadership of John Fitzgerald Kennedy, Jr. As the 35th president of the United States, JFK had a passion for public service, politics, his country, and his family. The museum and library give visitors a chance to see his legacy.

Joy Street

A notable street located in the Beacon Hill area of Boston. The African Meeting House as well as the headquarters for the Boston Chapter of the Appalachian Mountain Club (AMC) can be found along this street.

KENMORE SQUARE

Home to Fenway Park, Lansdowne Street, and the famous Citgo Sign.

KID POWER

An exhibit at the Boston Children's Museum designed to educate on health and fitness. Dance, climb the rock wall, and learn about nutrition in this fun interactive environment.

KING'S CHAPEL

A Christian Unitarian Church in Boston's Back Bay. The chapel is one of the historic sites along the Freedom Trail. The original church was made of wood, but was rebuilt in stone and finished in 1754. The church bell once cracked and was repaired by Paul Revere. It still rings at services today.

KING'S CHAPEL BURYING GROUND

For 30 years this was Boston's only burying ground and became the burial place for many historical figures. Located along the Freedom Trail, it sits on the land that was originally Isaac Johnson's vegetable garden. Isaac Johnson was the very first person to be buried here.

L

LIBERTY SCHOONER FLEET

The schooner *Liberty* and the schooner *Liberty Clipper*. Both vessels are replicas of 19th-century ships. The *Liberty* is 80 feet long and was modeled after the cargo carrying ships used by New England fishermen. The *Liberty Clipper* is 125 feet long and is a replica of a 19th-century clipper ship.

LION AND UNICORN

Emblems of British royalty that decorate the gables of the Old State House. On July 18, 1776 the Declaration of Independence was read aloud to the people of Boston from the balcony, and that evening the emblems were taken down. A lion and unicorn were returned to the façade in 1882.

LITTLE BREWSTER ISLAND

One of the islands found in Boston's outer harbor and the home to Boston Light.

LOBSTER

A staple to the commerce of New England, these crustaceans live at the bottom of the ocean, have two claws, and must molt their protective exoskeleton shell in order to grow. The James Hook & Company, in Boston, is a major lobster distributor. Founded in 1925, this family operated business continues to sell lobsters to fine restaurants around Boston, and New England.

Logan Airport

Massachusetts' major commercial airport. Logan Airport is located in East Boston. The airport's six runways are responsible for over 1,000 flights each day.

Long Wharf

Home to the Long Wharf Marriot, several shops and restaurants, and also next to the New England Aquarium. Long Wharf is where many of Boston's ferry boats, shuttles, whale watch cruises, and sightseeing tours depart from.

Longfellow Bridge

This bridge that crosses from Boston to Cambridge is also called the "Salt and Pepper Shaker Bridge," named after the towers along the bridge that resemble salt and pepper shakers. In addition to car traffic, the bridge also carries tens of thousands of subway passengers on the MBTA's Red Line each day. The bridge, named after Henry Wadsworth Longfellow, was opened in 1906 and is almost 1,800 feet long. It is said the architect was trying to compete with beautiful European bridges when he designed this bridge.

Longfellow National Historic Site

The home of American poet, Henry Wadsworth Longfellow, from 1837-1882, is located on Brattle Street in Cambridge. George Washington also used the home as his headquarters for nine months during the Revolutionary War. The home is now a museum and looks much like it did when Longfellow lived there.

Louisburg Square

Located on Beacon Hill. Louisburg Square has a grassy square with statues of Christopher Columbus and Aristides the Just.

M

Make Way for Ducklings

The official children's book of the Commonwealth of Massachusetts. *Make Way for Ducklings* was written and illustrated by Robert McCloskey and was first published in 1941. It tells the story of a pair of ducks who choose to raise their ducklings in Boston's Public Garden. The statues of the mother duck and her eight ducklings are now a favorite sight to see in the Public Garden.

Mamma Maria

An award-winning Italian restaurant in Boston's North End.

Mass Turnpike

One of Massachusetts' major highways and a part of Interstate 90. The Mass Pike is 138 miles long and stretches from East Boston to the New York border.

Massachusetts

One of the original 13 colonies and the sixth state to join the union. It is officially called the Commonwealth of Massachusetts. Massachusetts is a part of New England and is bordered by New York, Connecticut, Rhode Island, New Hampshire, Vermont, and the Atlantic Ocean. Although Massachusetts is one of the country's smallest states according to size, only 12 states have a larger population.

Massachusetts General Hospital

Usually called "Mass General," this hospital is the oldest and largest general hospital in New England and the third oldest in the country. The hospital conducts over 34,000 surgeries and admits over 45,000 patients each year.

Mayor Curley Statues

Two statues located in Faneuil Hall that honor James Michael Curley. One statue shows Mayor Curley sitting on a park bench, and the other statue stands just a few feet away and shows Mayor Curley standing up, wearing a campaign button, and most likely delivering a speech. James Michael Curley served as the Mayor of Boston for four terms, a member of the United States House of Representatives for two terms, and as the 35th Governor of Massachusetts.

MBTA

The Massachusetts Bay Transit Authority, or the MBTA, is the organization that controls most of the bus, train, subway, and ferry services in the Boston area. A logo with a capital letter T in a circle has given the service the short nickname "The T."

MEMORIAL DRIVE

The street that runs along the Cambridge side of the Charles River. On Sundays, between April and November, part of the road is closed to traffic and people enjoy rollerblading, dog walking, jogging, bicycling, and walking while enjoying the views.

MIDDLESEX COUNTY VOLUNTEERS

A fife and drum corps modeled after the ones that were a part of the American War for Independence. The group has over 60 performances a year and entertains audiences with their music while also educating audiences about history.

MILLENNIUM PARK

A 100-acre park in West Roxbury. The land was once the Gardner Street Dump but was filled in with dirt from the Big Dig. The park now has an amphitheater, six miles of trails, baseball fields, and picnic areas.

MINUTEMEN

A name given to the men of the Massachusetts militia who promised to be ready for service in a minutes notice. The Minutemen existed as early as 1645 and are probably best known for their contribution during the Revolutionary War.

MISSION CHURCH

A church in the Mission Hill area of Boston. The church is one of just 43 basilicas in the United States and was given that title in 1954 by Pope Pius XII. It is also the home to a world famous organ. The church's official name is Our Lady of Perpetual Help.

MIT

Massachusetts Institute of Technology. MIT is a university in Cambridge located very close to the Charles River. Teaching and research, with regard to practical application, continue to be this school's primary purpose.

MOUNTED POLICE

The division of the Boston Police Department that rides horseback. The horses are stabled at the Brandegee Estate.

Mural in Chinatown

A large painting on a brick building on Oak Street in Boston's Chinatown. The mural shows the history of the Chinese people in Boston.

Museum of Afro-American History

A museum dedicated to educating its visitors about the contributions of African Americans in New England beginning in colonial times. The museum is located on Beacon Hill in Boston and also on Nantucket.

Museum of Fine Arts

Often simply called the MFA, this museum is located on Huntington Avenue in Boston. The museum has the second largest permanent collection of art in the Americas. It was opened in 1876.

Museum of Science

Boston's science museum. The museum has over 500 interactive exhibits and is also home to the Mugar Omni IMAX Theater, the Hayden Planetarium, one of the world's largest Van De Graaff generators, and over 100 live animals.

Mystic River

A river that travels through Arlington, Medford, Somerville, Everett, Charlestown, Chelsea, and East Boston and then meets up with the Charles River to help form Boston's Inner Harbor.

Nantucket Lightship II

One of the lightships once stationed off of Nantucket to help guide ships safely around the island. Nantucket Lightship II was built in 1952 and was first stationed in the Ambrose Channel in New York. It later moved to Nantucket where it took turns with Nantucket Lightship I every 21 days. The lightship was decommissioned in 1985 has since been converted to a luxury ship and is available for charters in Boston from October through April.

National Park Service Rangers

The narrators who take visitors on tours of the Freedom Trail.

New England

The Northeast region of the United States. New England includes Maine, New Hampshire, Vermont, Massachusetts, Rhode Island, and Connecticut. Boston is considered the capital of New England.

New England Aquarium

An aquarium that was opened in 1969 with the world's largest circular saltwater tank. Since then the aquarium has continued to grow. It has recently added Boston's only 3D theater. It is home to a rescue and rehabilitation center that has helped over 4,000 marine animals since its opening.

New England Aquarium's Voyager III

A high speed catamaran belonging to the aquarium. The boat takes passengers to Stellwagen Bank to visit and learn about the whales that travel to the area each summer.

Nichols House Museum

A home built in 1804 that now serves as a museum on Beacon Hill. The house was home to the Nichols family and is preserved to show visitors what life was like in the 19th and 20th centuries for Bostonians living in the Beacon Hill area.

North End Market

The North End is an Italian community that is not only home to a large population of Italian residents, but also many Italian bakeries and restaurants. The North End markets provide fresh food to the restaurants and shops found there.

North Station

The terminal for the MBTA's northern train routes. Trains heading to or coming from the northern locations arrive and depart from this station. It is also a stop on the subway's Orange and Green Lines.

Newbury Street

A street in Boston's Back Bay known for its large number of shops and restaurants. Newbury Street is said to be one of the most expensive streets in the United States.

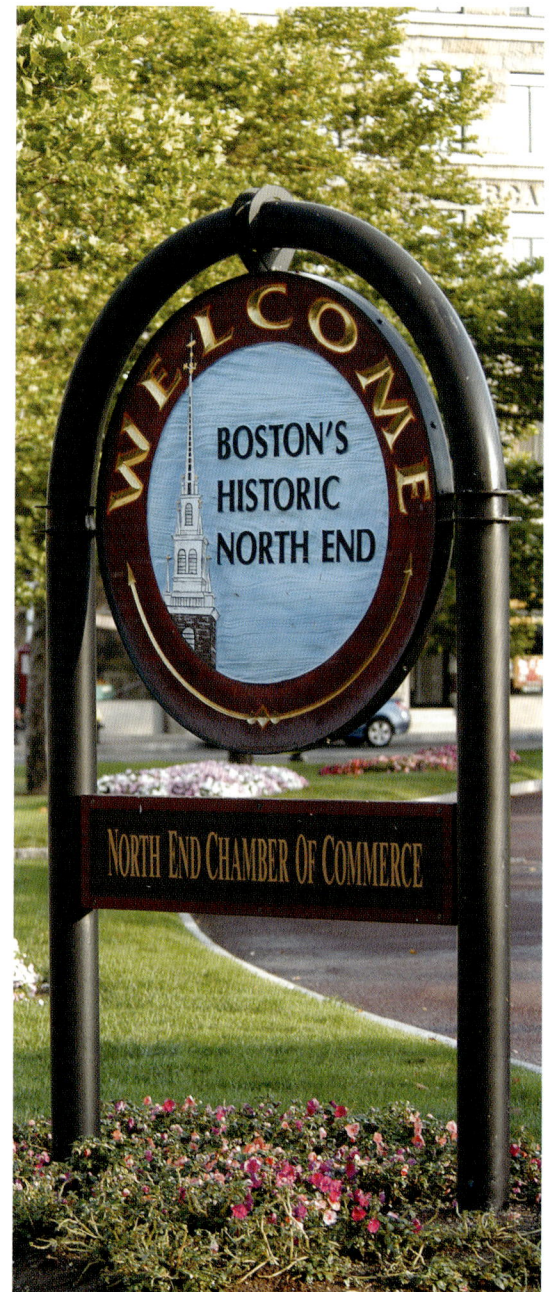

Odyssey Cruises

A luxurious way to cruise Boston Harbor and view the skyline by boat. The ship has three enclosed decks so trips can be run in all types of weather. Passengers can sightsee while also enjoying food, live entertainment, and dancing.

Old City Hall

Located on School Street in Boston, this building housed the City Council from 1965-1969. The building is now used for office space and even has a steak house restaurant in it. It is a United States National Historic Landmark and is on the Freedom Trail.

Old Corner Bookstore

Built in 1712, this is one of the oldest structures in Boston. It is located along the Freedom Trail at the corner of School and Washington Streets. Anne Hutchinson lived in the original building. It was known as the Crease House and the Brimmer Mansion, but it wasn't until much later that it was actually used as a bookstore. Publishers Ticknor and Fields worked out of the building, and many famous authors and poets such as Henry Wadsworth Longfellow, Charles Dickens, and Henry David Thoreau passed through its doors.

Old North Church

The oldest active church building in Boston. The Old North Church is a Historic Landmark most commonly known for the part it played in Paul Revere's "midnight ride." Two lanterns were hung in the church's steeple and were lit to help spread the word about the advancing of British Troops. The saying goes, "One if by land, two if by sea." The Old North Church is on Salem Street in Boston's North End.

The Freedom Trail ← OLD NORTH CHURCH

Old South Church

A church built in 1873, for a congregation founded in 1669, still stands on Boylston Street in Boston. On top of the church is a 246-foot tower that houses its 2,020-pound bell. Famous members of the church included Samuel Adams and Benjamin Franklin.

Old South Meeting House

Now a museum and a National Historic Landmark, the Old South Meeting House was originally a Congregational church and was where the Boston Tea Party was organized on December 16, 1773. At the time the building was the largest in Boston. The steeple that still stands on top of the building is 183 feet tall. You can see this beautiful historic building as you walk along Boston's Freedom Trail.

Old State House

A historic landmark along the Freedom Trail. Built in 1713, it is the oldest standing public building in Boston. It was the seat of Massachusetts state government until 1798 when the new state house was put into use. Now a museum uses the building and it is a popular place for couples to get married.

Old Town Trolley Tours

A popular sightseeing tour that reveals the history of Boston to tourists and locals alike. With 18 stops and the ability for passengers to hop on and off at leisure, Old Town Trolley Tours are an enjoyable way to become familiar with the city.

Olmstead, Fredrick Law

An American landscape architect who designed The Emerald Necklace in Boston and many other famous parks throughout the country.

P

Park Street Church

An active Congregational Church founded in 1809 and a stop on the Freedom Trail. Most of the 26 people who founded the Park Street Church were former members of the Old South Meeting House. It is located on the corner of Tremont and Park Streets, but with a 217-foot-high steeple it can be seen from blocks away. This is also the site where *My Country 'Tis of Thee* was first sung.

Patriots

New England's professional National Football League team. The New England Patriots play home games at Gillette Stadium in Foxboro, Massachusetts.

Patriots Day

A holiday that honors the Battles of Lexington and Concord and the beginning of the Revolutionary War. The battles took place on April 19, 1775 and are reenacted each year at Lexington Green in Lexington and Minute Man National Historic park in Concord.

Penguins

Over 60 penguins belonging to three different species can be visited at the New England Aquarium. African penguins, found in South Africa, are known to be very loud, making noises that sound like the braying of a donkey. The African penguin has been on exhibit at the New England Aquarium since it opened in 1969. The little blue penguin is the smallest of all the penguin species. It will grow to a height of about 8 inches and weigh about 2 pounds. Originating from Australia, their scientific name, *Eudyptula minor*, means "good little diver." The rockhopper penguins are experts at jumping from rock to rock. Found in South America, the rockhopper penguin is vulnerable in the wild in large part due to habitat loss.

Piers Park

A 6.5-acre park on Marginal Street in Boston. The park includes a pier, shaded play areas, walkways, picnic areas, playgrounds, a lighthouse-shaped pavilion, and the Piers Park Sailing Center.

Paul Revere House

The oldest residence in downtown Boston. It became home to Paul Revere in 1770. Five years later on April 18th, Paul Revere left from this home to begin his famous midnight ride. The home is now a museum where visitors can see examples of Paul Revere's silver work and a 900-pound bronze bell cast in his foundry.

Planetarium

A favorite part of the Museum of Science. The Charles Hayden Planetarium uses a curved ceiling and powerful lasers to recreate the night sky. Different shows are offered to educate visitors about our universe, solar systems, constellations, planets, moons, stars, gravity, and space.

Powder Monkey

The person who is responsible for getting gunpowder to the gunner during battles. Boys as young as eight years old had this responsibility during the Revolutionary War.

Prescott, Colonel William

An American Colonel in the Revolutionary War. During the Battle of Bunker Hill, Colonel Prescott told his forces, "Do not fire until you see the whites of their eyes." A statue of Colonel Prescott stands on Bunker Hill in Charlestown.

Prudential Center

A large building in Boston's Back Bay area that is a combination of apartments, office space, and retail stores with over 75 shops and restaurants. The Prudential Tower is 52 stories high and is the second-tallest building in Boston.

Public Garden

A 24-acre park that was the first botanical garden in the United States. In 1859 the Massachusetts Legislature decided the Public Garden should be preserved forever. Many of the flowers enjoyed throughout the park are grown in greenhouses around the city and are replanted once in full bloom to help make sure the garden is always full of beautiful colors.

Puritans

A group of Protestants from England who left their native land and headed for the New World in search of religious freedom. In the 1600s these Puritans settled in New England. They first settled in Salem, moved to Charlestown, and finally ended up in Boston in 1630.

Quarterdeck

An area of a ship commonly reserved for officers and ceremonial functions. Usually the Commanding Officer will issue his/her commands from the quarterdeck.

Quick Facts

Boston was founded on September 17, 1630.

Boston is 48 square miles in size.

Boston has a population of nearly 600,000 in the city and about 4 million in the surrounding metro region or Greater Boston.

The average winter temperature is 36 degrees and the average summer temperature is 82 degrees.

Boston is in a temperate region, which means it experiences four different seasons each year.

Boston has the first public park, the first public library, the first public school, and the first subway.

Quincy Market

A historic building that is a part of Faneuil Hall Marketplace. The building was finished in 1826 and named after Mayor Josiah Quincy. The long rectangular building is home to a large food court serving everything from pastries to pizza and seafood to sorbet. The two outer halls are full of vending carts that sell a large variety of gifts, toys, souvenirs, and clothes.

R

Red Coats

The name given to British soldiers during the Revolutionary War. The soldiers were given the name because of the red coats that were a part of their uniforms.

Red Sox

New England's professional Major League Baseball team. The Boston Red Sox started in 1901 and have been a part of baseball's American League ever since. The teams' name was given to them by then owner John I. Taylor in 1907. You can see the red and blue banners that represent all of their American League and World Series Championship wins if you visit Fenway Park. Fenway has been their home ballpark since 1912 and it is the oldest professional ballpark in America.

Revere, Paul

A silversmith and craftsman most famous for playing the role of messenger in the Battles of Lexington and Concord. On the night of April 18, 1775, Dr. Joseph Warren told Paul Revere to ride from Boston, across the Charles River to Charlestown, and eventually on to Lexington to warn patriots about the advancement of the British troops. Paul Revere had told the sexton at the Old North Church to light one lantern if the British were coming by land or two lanterns if they were advancing by sea. Legend says that Paul Revere shouted, "The British are coming!" during his famous midnight ride, but he actually was a bit more discreet and yelled something more to the effect of "the regulars are coming out!"

Revolution, the New England

New England's professional Major League Soccer team. The New England Revolution play their home games at Gillette Stadium in Foxboro, Massachusetts. The team was founded in October of 1995 and began its first season in 1996. The Revolution won their first MLS Cup in 2002.

Sailing

A popular activity that takes place on the Charles River or Boston Harbor. Lessons are given and boats can be rented for a day of fun.

Rose Fitzgerald Kennedy Greenway

Thirty acres of parks and green space that stretch from Chinatown, through the Wharf District, the North End, and to the Fleet Center. Dedicated to Rose Kennedy on July 26, 2004, it was officially opened with a large celebration in October of 2007.

Rotary

A traffic circle where several different roads enter at different points around a central island. Visitors to Boston are often bewildered by the presence of rotaries and the locals commonly poke fun at them. Causing confusion, they are dreaded by those who are not accustomed to driving through them. It is said Boston has more rotaries than any other place in the country.

Rowes Wharf

Home to the Boston Harbor Hotel, a marina, commuter boats, harbor cruise boats, and a floating dock that offers movies and concerts during the summer.

Sargent, John Singer

John Singer Sargent was an artist who lived from 1856-1925. He is mostly remembered as a portrait artist, but in Boston he is most famous for the murals that he painted in the Boston Public Library.

Science Playground

An interactive exhibit at the Boston Children's Museum. Children investigate the natural world while developing questioning skills as they incorporate all of their senses.

Seabiscuit

A champion thoroughbred racehorse discovered at Suffolk Downs racetrack in Boston. Amongst many other major wins, Seabiscuit won the Massachusetts Handicap in 1937.

Seaport Belle

One of the many vessels run by Boston Yacht Charters. The *Seaport Belle* is a steamship replica and offers harbor tours for up to 149 passengers.

Shaw, Robert Gould

A colonel in the American Civil War who was in command of the all-black 54th Massachusetts Volunteer Infantry. A memorial stands in his honor at Beacon and Park Streets, across from the State House.

Shawmut

The peninsula now known as Boston was originally called Shawmut Point. Between 1631 and 1890 Boston tripled in size when surrounding hills were cut down and marshes, ponds, and waterfront along the peninsula were filled in with the soil.

Shirley Eustis House

A historic home built in Roxbury during the mid 1700s by William Shirley. Shirley was the Royal Governor of the Massachusetts Bay Colony, and the Commander-in-Chief of the British forces in North America. It was later home to a Federal Governor named William Eustis. The home is now open for tours.

Skyline

A view of a city's tallest buildings. Different buildings are seen in Boston's skyline depending from where you are looking. Some of the buildings you are most likely to see are the John Hancock Tower, the Prudential Tower, the Federal Reserve Bank, One Boston Place, One International Place, Two International Place, 111 Huntington Avenue, and Exchange Place.

Soldiers and Sailors Monument

Located in Boston Common, this 126-foot, granite monument was dedicated to the soldiers and sailors who died during the U.S. Civil War.

South Boston

A neighborhood in Boston commonly called "Southie."

South Boston St. Patrick's Day Parade

South Boston has a mostly Irish-American population and has been celebrating a St. Patrick's Day party and parade for over 100 years beginning in 1901.

South End

A neighborhood in Boston home to great restaurants, lots of shopping, beautiful brownstone buildings, and over 30 parks.

South Station

Boston's largest train station and bus terminal. MBTA subways and commuter rail trains, Amtrak trains, and the high-speed Acela Express run out of South Station along with Boston's inter-city buses.

Spectacle Island

One of the islands that comprise Boston Harbor Islands National Park. Spectacle Island provides a marina, visitor center, walking trails, beaches, and incredible views of Boston Harbor for sightseers to enjoy.

Stamp Act of 1765

An act passed by the Parliament of Great Britain stating all newspapers, legal documents, contracts, pamphlets, and even playing cards had to carry a stamp tax to be paid by the American colonists. The colonists were furious with this decision and many tax collectors were not willing to put themselves in danger by trying to collect the taxes. The act was repealed almost exactly one year later.

State House

The seat of government for the Commonwealth of Massachusetts. The offices of the Governor and state legislature are located within the State House. The building was designed by Charles Bulfinch and was built in 1787 on pasture land belonging to John Hancock. The State House is one of the many historic sites along Boston's Freedom Trail.

Spirit of Massachusetts

Modeled after the fast and reliable 1889 fishing schooner *Fredonia*, the *Spirit of Massachusetts* was launched at Charlestown Navy Yard in 1984. Intended to be used as a training vessel, she was purchased by the Ocean Classroom Foundation to teach young people how to sail.

Sports Museum of New England

A collection of sports' memorabilia honoring the teams and athletes that have represented New England over the years. The museum's purpose is not only to entertain sports enthusiasts, but they also hope to educate the children who visit while instilling the values of leadership, respect, and cooperation. You can visit the museum at the TD Banknorth Garden.

Storrow Drive

Officially named the James Jackson Storrow Memorial Drive, this road is a major expressway that runs along the east-side banks of the Charles River. Because it is a parkway, large trucks and buses are not allowed to drive on it.

Street Performer

Musicians, jugglers, magicians, and mimes entertain visitors for pocket change throughout Boston but are commonly found in Harvard Square and around Quincy Market.

Sumner Tunnel

A tunnel that runs traffic under Boston Harbor from Logan Airport and East Boston to the North End. The Sumner Tunnel runs parallel to the Callahan Tunnel, which allows traffic to flow in the opposite direction.

Swan

Large water birds related to geese and ducks. Swans have lived in Boston's Public Garden for years and their return each spring is a much anticipated event.

Swan Boats

Found nowhere else in the world, these famous boats are paddled around Boston's Public Garden each summer. Inventor Robert Paget was inspired by the German opera, *Lohengrin* in which a knight crosses a river in a boat pulled by a swan. Over 120 years later, the Pagent family continues to offer tours of the lagoon.

T

Tall Ships

18th and 19th-century sailing ships whose masts are made in segments. In 1992 and 2000 over 100 tall ships sailed into Boston Harbor as part of a four-month race. The ships spent four days in the city and participated in Sail Boston and the Parade of Sails. People could see the ships at the docks, in the harbor, and under full sail.

TD Banknorth Garden

Home to the Boston Celtics, the Boston Bruins, and the Sports Museum of New England. The TD Banknorth Garden also hosts concerts, ice shows, circuses, and other events each year.

Tea Act of 1773

An act that allowed the East India Tea Company to export tea to the American colonies without having to pay duties or taxes.

Tea Pot

A 200-pound tea kettle that can be found hanging over a retail space at the intersection of Tremont and Court Streets. The teapot, which is continuously steaming, was made in 1873 by the Oriental Tea Company, who had a contest to guess the capacity of the large kettle. The correct answer was 227 gallons, 2 quarts, 1 pint, and 3 gills.

Ted Williams Tunnel

A tunnel that runs under Boston Harbor and connects traffic between South Boston to Logan Airport in East Boston. This tunnel was part of the Big Dig Project and was opened to commercial traffic in 1995 and all other traffic in 2003. It is named after the legendary Red Sox player, Ted Williams.

Theater District

An area in Boston home to a variety of theaters such as the Wang, the Shubert, and the Colonial. Musicals, plays, ballets, concerts, and comedy shows can be seen throughout the year at the different locations. The theater district also has many restaurants.

Thermopylae Sculpture

A 16-foot-high bronze sculpture located in front of the Kennedy Federal Building. *Thermopylae* was created in the modernist style by sculptor Dimitri Hadzi.

Tobin Bridge

The Maurice J. Tobin Memorial Bridge, named after a former Boston Mayor and Massachusetts Governor, was formerly called the Mystic River Bridge. It crosses high above the Mystic River and connects Chelsea to Charlestown. Southbound traffic travels on the upper part of the bridge while northbound traffic travels on the lower level.

Tortoise and Hare

Bronze sculptures created by Nancy Schön that sit on bricks in Copley Square, near the finish line of the Boston Marathon. The *Tortoise and Hare* were created to celebrate the 100th running of the Boston Marathon and are meant to represent the large variety of runners who participate in the race each year.

Townshend Acts of 1767

Acts proposed by Charles Townshend and passed by Parliament that made colonists pay new taxes on lead, paint, paper, glass, and tea.

Triceratops

A part of the Museum of Science's Dinosaurs: Modeling the Mesozoic exhibit. Here you can examine bones and footprints which provide evidence of the Triceratops.

Trinity Church

A beautiful Episcopal church located in the Back Bay of Boston. The church was founded in 1733 and the congregation now has about 3,000 households. Trinity Church stands next to the John Hancock Building on pilings that are deeply sunk into Boston Harbor.

Tugboats

The small and very powerful boats that help guide large ships into the harbor by either towing or pushing them along.

Tyrannosaurus Rex

The Museum of Science's Dinosaurs: Modeling the Mesozoic exhibit is a favorite. Standing in the center of this exhibit is a full sized Tyrannosaurus Rex. Paleontologists have found over 30 skeletons and have used those to build the complete and giant T-Rex.

U.S. Post Office

Created in 1775 by the Second Continental Congress under Benjamin Franklin. By 1971 the department was reorganized as a semi-independent agency of the federal government. Today, post offices can be found throughout every town and city in the United States.

Union Oyster House

The oldest restaurant in Boston and the one restaurant that has remained in business longer than any other in the United States. The Union Oyster House opened in 1826 and can be found on Union Street around the corner from Faneuil Hall.

USS Cassin Young

This Fletcher-Class destroyer is a versatile combat ship built for WWII. Instrumental in the rescue of other men from sinking vessels, escorting other ships to their destination, and fending off kamikaze pilots, the USS *Cassin Young* is now a museum run by the National Park Service and can be found in the Charlestown Navy Yard.

USS Constitution & Museum

A wooden-hulled frigate belonging to the United States Navy. The hull of the USS *Constitution* was made from 2,000 live oak trees and was nicknamed "Old Ironsides" because of how well she stood up during a skirmish with a ship called *Guerriere* during the War of 1812. She is now the oldest commissioned ship still afloat in the world. The ship and museum are located in the Charlestown Navy Yard along Boston's historic Freedom Trail.

Van de Graaff generator

The Museum of Science in Boston is the owner of the world's largest Van de Graaff generator. It is on display in the *Thomson Theatre of Electricity* with daily demonstrations to show off its enormous electrical power. Giant sparks that look more like lightning are created from the high voltage, which puts on quite a show.

Victory Gardens

Gardens that were planted throughout the country during World War II. President Roosevelt asked Americans to plant their own fruit and vegetable gardens in order to help alleviate shortages due to the War. The Fenway Victory Gardens were the last of all of the Victory Gardens planted.

Victura

A 26-foot Wianno Senior sailboat that was given to JFK by his parents on his 15th birthday. It is now on display at the JFK Library.

Wadsworth House

The headquarters of the Harvard Alumni Association on the campus of Harvard University.

Wally The Green Monster

The mascot of the Boston Red Sox. Wally is named after the big green wall in Fenway Park's left field. Wally became a part of the team in 1997 and appears at every home game.

Washington, George

The Commander-in-Chief of the American army beginning in 1775, the first President of the United States from 1789-1797, and Lieutenant General in 1798. Washington was honored with the title of General after his death. Washington lived in Cambridge for nine months, at what is now the Henry Wadsworth Longfellow House, while he victoriously forced the British out of Boston. There is a statue of George Washington on horseback in the Boston Public Garden.

WATERFRONT

The part of Boston that sits upon Boston Harbor. Some of Boston's waterfront preserves the history of the city while other parts are giving it new life. Hotels, the Aquarium, charter boats, shops, restaurants, parks, the Children's Museum, and the Boston Tea Party Ship are just some of the things you'll find along Boston's waterfront today.

WHALE WATCH

A boat trip that leaves daily during nice weather to visit the whales on Stellwagen Bank or Jeffrey's Ledge, off the coast of Massachusetts.

White, Mayor Kevin

Kevin Hagen White was the longest serving mayor in Boston. His term lasted from 1968 to 1984. Perhaps White's biggest success was to reopen Quincy Market, revitalizing Boston's downtown. A statue of this influential former mayor stands along Congress Street near Faneuil Hall.

Winthrop Park

The oldest park in Cambridge. Winthrop Park is on the outskirts of Harvard Square. The park, originally Winthrop Square back in the 1600s, was a marketplace where local farmers sold their produce. In 1846 it was fenced in and made into a small park that can still be enjoyed today.

Winthrop, John

John Winthrop came to Massachusetts in 1630 and became the first governor of the Massachusetts Colony.

X, Y, Z

IMAX

Short for Image Maximum, IMAX theaters use giant screens that are usually a few stories high to create the best quality images. Omnimax theaters actually use rounded surfaces to make the quality even one step better. The Mugar Omni Theater at the Museum of Science has a five-story-tall IMAX Dome. The New England Aquarium also has an IMAX theater.

YAWKEY WAY

A street that lines one side of Fenway Park. Yawkey Way is named after past team owner Tom Yawkey and is now closed off during games for ticketed fans only. Eating a sausage or hotdog on Yawkey Way has become a part of the Fenway experience. Fans can also watch sports announcers during live shows at Jerry Remy's outdoor restaurant, Rem Dawgs.

ZAKIM BUNKER HILL MEMORIAL BRIDGE

The world's widest cable-stayed bridge. The Zakim Bridge was completed in 2003 as part of the "Big Dig" and is named after a civic leader from Boston, Leonard P. Zakim, and the Battle of Bunker Hill. It is said the white cables were made to look like the sails of the USS *Constitution*. At night the bridge shines with a beautiful blue glow.

Been There, Done That!

STICKER SHEET

Now that you've seen the historic monuments, learned all the interesting facts, and visited the fun attractions of Boston, it's time to mark where you've been and what you've done. Simply match the places on the stickers to their correct location on the map to create your own personal guide around Boston.

The State House

Paul Revere House

New England Aquarium

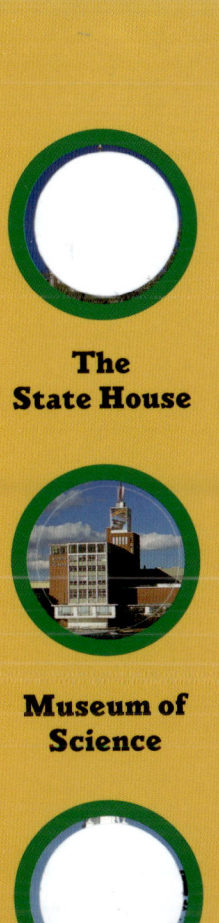
Faneuil Hall Marketplace

Museum of Science

Boston Public Garden

Boston Common

The North End

Old North Church

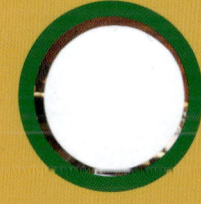
Hatch Memorial Shell

Christopher Columbus Park

Granary Burial Ground

Bunker Hill Monument

U.S.S. Constitution

Boston Duck Tour

Fenway Park